Anthology of Jewish Art Song
Volume II

Father To Son:
A Hugo Chaim Adler and Samuel Adler Solo Collection

Anthology of Jewish Art Song, Volume II
Father To Son: A Hugo Chaim Adler and Samuel Adler Solo Collection
993357

A Division of URJ Books and Music
633 Third Avenue, New York, NY 10017
www.TranscontinentalMusic.com
www.URJBooksAndMusic.com

This book is printed on acid-free paper.
Manufactured in the United States of America
ISBN-10: 0-8074-1129-2
ISBN-13: 978-0-8074-1129-2
10 9 8 7 6 5 4 3 2 1

Anthology of
Jewish Art Song
Volume II

Father To Son:
A Hugo Chaim Adler and Samuel Adler Solo Collection

Editors
Jayson Rodovsky
Michael Boxer

Project Manager and Typesetter
Joshua Wiczer

Transcontinental Music Publications
New York, NY

PREFACE

It is a special privilege for me to have Transcontinental Music publish an album of songs which contains works of both my father and my own. Ever since I was very young, my father was my inspiration as well as my life model. Being a fine pianist, he accompanied my violin playing daily from the time I was able to play major works on the instrument. This was the foundation of my musical education. Later in life, we became even closer, much more like best friends and colleagues rather than father and son. He gloried in my every undertaking and urged me on in every endeavor of my life. That we can share a volume of songs is a dream for me and a constant reminder how much his life and achievement meant to me.

My father was mostly self-taught in composition, except for a short two years of study with Ernst Toch. When I was studying harmony and counterpoint in college, he worked out every assignment I was given at both Boston University and at Harvard. This was a great thrill for him and gave him a new lease on life at moments when he was quite ill with cancer. My father, in later years, would never publish a work without my "approval", though I seldom, if ever, criticized it. He always said that it made him feel better to have me like the work. Unfortunately, he was taken from us much too soon, and I think that I speak for the entire family when I say that we all miss him every day. His vision of music for the synagogue was most idealistic for he felt it should only be music of the highest quality, and tried all his life to live up to that ideal.

I want to dedicate this volume to him and to my dear mother who was his helpmate for so many years. May their memories be a blessing for all of us.

– *Samuel Adler*

SAMUEL ADLER was born March 4, 1928 in Mannheim, Germany and came to the United States in 1939. Inducted into the American Academy of Arts and Letters in May 2001, Adler is the composer of over 400 published works, including five operas, six symphonies, twelve concerti, eight string quartets, four oratorios, and many other orchestral, band, chamber and choral works and songs, which have been performed all over the world. He is also the author of three books: *Choral Conducting* (Holt, Reinhart and Winston 1971, second edition Schirmer Books 1985), *Sight Singing* (W.W. Norton 1979, 1997) and *The Study of Orchestration* (W.W. Norton 1982, 1989, 2001). He has also contributed numerous articles to major magazines and books published in the United States and abroad.

Adler was educated at Boston University and Harvard University, and holds four honorary doctorates from Southern Methodist University, Wake Forest University, St. Mary's Notre-Dame, and the St. Louis Conservatory. His major teacher in conducting was Serge Koussevitsky, and in composition were Herbert Fromm, Walter Piston, Randall Thompson, Paul Hindemith and Aaron Copland.

He is Professor Emeritus at the Eastman School of Music, where he taught from 1966 to 1995 and served as chair of the Composition Department from 1974 until his retirement. Before going to Eastman, Adler served as professor of composition at the University of North Texas. He was Music Director at Temple Emanu-El in Dallas, Texas from 1953 to 1966, Instructor of Fine Arts at the Hockaday School in Dallas, Texas from 1955 to 1966, and Music Director of the Dallas Lyric Theater and the Dallas Chorale from 1954 to 1958. Since 1997, he has been a member of the composition faculty at the Julliard School of Music in New York City. Adler has given master classes and workshops at over 300 universities worldwide, and in the summers has taught at major music festivals such as Tanglewood, Aspen, Brevard and Bowdoin, as well as others in France, Germany, Israel, Spain, Austria, Poland, South America and Korea.

Adler has appeared as conductor with many major symphony orchestras, both in the United States and abroad. His compositions are published by Theodore Presser, Oxford University Press, G. Schirmer, Carl Fischer, E.C. Schirmer, Peters Edition, Ludwig Music, Southern Music Publishers and Transcontinental Music Publications, and have been recorded on Naxos, Gasparo, Albany, CRI, Crystal, Vanguard and others.

Adler has been awarded many prizes, including a 1990 award from the American Academy of Arts and Letters, the Charles Ives Award, the Lillian Fairchild Award, the MTNA award for Composer of the Year (1988-1989), and citation by the American Federation of Music Clubs (2001). In 1983, he won the Deems Taylor Award for his book, *The Study of Orchestration.* In 1989, he was designated "Phi Beta Kappa Scholar" and received the Eastman School's Eisenhard Award for distinguished teaching. In 1991, he was named Composer of the Year by the American Guild of Organists. Adler was awarded a Guggenheim Fellowship (1975-1976), was a MacDowell Fellow for five years, and was elected to the Chilean Academy of Fine Arts for his "outstanding contribution to the world of music as a composer" during his second visit to Chile in 1993. In 1999, he was elected to the Akademie der Kuenste in Germany for distinguished service to music. While serving in the United States Army (1950-1952), Adler founded and conducted the Seventh Army Symphony Orchestra, and because of the orchestra's great psychological and musical impact on European culture, he was awarded the Army's Medal of Honor. In May of 2003, Adler was awarded the Aaron Copland Award by the American Society of Composers, Authors and Publishers for lifetime achievement in composition and teaching on the occasion of his 75th birthday. In November of 2008, Samuel Adler was inducted into the American Classical Music Hall of Fame.

HUGO CHAIM ADLER, an American cantor and composer, was born in 1894 in Antwerp, Belgium, and died in 1955 in Worcester, Massachusetts. He attended the Jewish Teachers' Seminary in Cologne, Germany, graduating in 1917, the Conservatories of Cologne in 1917 and the Conservatories of Frankurt from 1915 to 1916, in addition to private compositional studie with Ernst Toch from 1924 to 1926. In 1922, he became cantor of the chief synagogue in Mannheim, Germany, where he remained until his emigration to the United States in January of 1939. From 1927 to 1939, he was extremely active in the Kulturbund movement in Germany and wrote many works for performances all over Europe and what was then Palestine. Some of the most successful of these were *Licht Und Volk* (1928), revised later in the United States under the new title *Bearers of Light* (1954); *To Zion* (1930); *Job* (1932); *Balak and Balaam* (1934, revised 1948); *Shirah Chadasha* (1936); *Akedah* (1938); and *Ten German Songs* (1936).

After his arrival in the United States, Adler became cantor and music director of Temple Emanuel in Worcester, Massachusetts, where he continued to write music for the synagogue. In 1942, he was awarded first place by the Central Conference of American Rabbis for his *Music of the Synagogue*, a collection of settings of liturgical texts for the 1940 *Union Prayer Book.* Besides many other liturgical settings, he wrote larger cantatas: *Jonah* (1944); *Behold The Jew* (1945); *A Parable Against Persecution* (1947); and two complete services: *Avodath Habonim* (1943) and *Nachlath Israel* (1952). Adler also had a great interest in preserving the musical heritage of the Jews of southern Germany and arranged quite a few of their traditional tunes for use in the American synagogue.

Table of Contents

In memory of Sarah Tankus Weinberger

High Voice

A Woman of Valor

(Eishet Chayil)

Proverbs 31:20, 28-30

Samuel Adler

Andantino (♩ = 58)
Voice
Keyboard
mf
mp
A wo-man of val - or who can find?
V.
Kybd.
Her price is far a-bove ru - bies. Her child-ren rise up, and call her
blessed; her hus - band al - so, and he prais - es her. Man - y daughters

V.
Kybd.
have done val-iant-ly, But thou ex - cel-lest them all.
Grace is de-ceit-ful, and
beau-ty is vain; but a wo - man that fear-eth the Lord,
she shall be prais - ed,
she shall be prais-ed, she shall be prais - ed.
molto ritard

Originally published upon the 10th Yahrzeit of Hugo Ch. Adler (1894 - 1955)
To A. Albert Klein in blessed memory

Adonai Mah Adam

(O God, What is Man?)

Psalms 144: 3, 4; 90: 6, 3
Deuteronomy 32: 29
Psalms 49:18; 37:37; 34:23

Hugo Ch. Adler

Note: This piece was originally written for organ. Leave off the lower octave of the left hand, when necessary.

tenuto
un poco mosso
mf
e - rev, la - e - rev y'-mo-leil v'-ya - veish. Ta-
f
sheiv e-nosh ad da - ka, va - to - mer: "shu - vu,
ff
mf
poco ritard
Tempo I°
tenuto
shu-vu v'-nei a-dam!" Lu chach-mu yas - ki - lu zot, va-vi - nu, ya-
pp
poco ritard
poco lento
vi-nu l'-a - cha - ri - tam. Ki lo v'-mo-to yi-kach ha-kol, lo
V.
Kybd.

35
ritard
A Tempo
tenuto
V.
yei-reid a-cha-rav k'-vo - do. Sh'-mar-tam, u-r'-ai ya-shar,
Kybd.
39
ki a-cha-rit l'-ish sha-lom; po-deh A-do-nai ne-fesh a-
42
tenuto
Tempo I°
va - dav; v'-lo ye - sh'-mu, v'-lo ye - sh'-mu kol ha-cho-
45
ritard
sim bo, kol ha-cho - sim bo.

יְהוָה מָה־אָדָם וַתֵּדָעֵהוּ בֶּן־אֱנוֹשׁ וַתְּחַשְּׁבֵהוּ,
אָדָם לַהֶבֶל דָּמָה יָמָיו כְּצֵל עוֹבֵר!
בַּבֹּקֶר יָצִיץ וְחָלָף לָעֶרֶב יְמוֹלֵל וְיָבֵשׁ.
תָּשֵׁב אֱנוֹשׁ עַד־דַּכָּא וַתֹּאמֶר "שׁוּבוּ בְנֵי־אָדָם!"
לוּ חָכְמוּ יַשְׂכִּילוּ זֹאת יָבִינוּ לְאַחֲרִיתָם.
כִּי לֹא בְמוֹתוֹ יִקַּח הַכֹּל לֹא־יֵרֵד אַחֲרָיו כְּבוֹדוֹ.
שְׁמָר־תָּם וּרְאֵה יָשָׁר כִּי־אַחֲרִית לְאִישׁ שָׁלוֹם.
פּוֹדֶה יְהוָה נֶפֶשׁ עֲבָדָיו וְלֹא יֶאְשְׁמוּ כָּל־הַחֹסִים בּוֹ.

O Lord, what is man that You should care about him,
mortal man, that You should think of him,
man is like a breath; his days are like a passing shadow. At daybreak it flourishes anew; by dusk it withers and dries up. You return man to dust; You decreed, "Return you mortals!" Were they wise, they would think upon this, gain insight into their future. For when he dies he can take none of it along; his good cannot follow him down. Mark the blameless, note the upright, for there is a future for the man of integrity. The Lord redeems the life of His servants; all who take refuge in Him shall not be ruined.

High Voice

Ahavat Olam

(Everlasting Love)

Liturgy

Samuel Adler

V.
Kybd.
mei-nu na-si-ach b'-chu-ke-cha, v'-nis-mach b'-div-rei to-ra-te-cha uv'-mitz-vo-te-cha
l'-o-lam va-ed. Ki heim cha-yei-nu v'-o-rech ya-mei-nu u-va-
hem ne-h'-geh yo-mam va-lai-lah. V'-a-ha-va-t'-cha
al ta-sir mi-me-nu l'-o-la-mim. Ba-ruch a-tah, A-do-

אַהֲבַת עוֹלָם בֵּית יִשְׂרָאֵל עַמְּךָ אָהָבְתָּ,
תּוֹרָה וּמִצְוֹת, חֻקִּים וּמִשְׁפָּטִים, אוֹתָנוּ לִמַּדְתָּ.
עַל כֵּן יְיָ אֱלֹהֵינוּ, בְּשָׁכְבֵנוּ וּבְקוּמֵנוּ נָשִׂיחַ בְּחֻקֶּיךָ,
וְנִשְׂמַח בְּדִבְרֵי תוֹרָתֶךָ וּבְמִצְוֹתֶיךָ לְעוֹלָם וָעֶד.
כִּי הֵם חַיֵּינוּ וְאֹרֶךְ יָמֵינוּ, וּבָהֶם נֶהְגֶּה יוֹמָם וָלָיְלָה.
וְאַהֲבָתְךָ אַל תָּסִיר מִמֶּנּוּ לְעוֹלָמִים.
בָּרוּךְ אַתָּה יְיָ, אוֹהֵב עַמּוֹ יִשְׂרָאֵל.

Everlasting love You offered Your people Israel
by teaching us Torah and mitzvot, laws and precepts.
Therefore, Adonai our God,
when we lie down and when we rise up,
we will meditate on Your laws and Your commandments.
We will rejoice in Your Torah for ever.
Day and night we will reflect on them
for they are our life and doing them lengthens our days.
Never remove Your love from us.
Praise to You, Adonai, who loves Your people Israel.

High Voice

Bitte

(Plea)

German translation (from original Yiddish) by Albert Ehrenstein
English setting by Samuel Rosenbaum

Hugo Ch. Adler

Molto moderato
Keyboard
mf
p
calmo
p
V.
Mein Le - ben hängt von Nacht zu Nacht, von Schlaf
I like my life from night to night, from sleep
Kybd.
ritard
pp
zu Schlaf, von Nacht zu Nacht, von Schlaf zu Schlaf, von
to sleep, from night to night, from sleep to sleep, from

12
V.
pp
diminuendo
Traum zu Traum, von Traum zu
dream to dream, from dream to
Kybd.
diminuendo
16
Piu lento e maestoso
f
Traum.
O rafft mich
dream.
O do not
p
molto crescendo
ff
poco ritard
f
8vb
20
nicht aus mir em - por, o rafft mich nicht aus mir em -
wake me out of my dream, o do not wake me out of my
8vb

molto diminuendo
A tempo
V.
por, ich bin, ich bin im Schlaf so froh.
dream, I am filled with joy in my dreams.
Kybd.
Un poco piu mosso
Ich bin im Schlaf so froh. Ich
In my dreams I am filled with joy. In my
(leggiere)
bin im Schlaf so froh.
dreams I am filled with joy.

V.
(filled with joy, filled with joy, filled with joy, filled with joy)
Kybd.
p
pp
V.
Ich bin im Schlaf so froh.
I am filled with joy, in my dreams.
Ich
In my
Kybd.
V.
bin im Schlaf so froh.
dreams, I dream of joy.
Ich bin im Schlaf so froh.
In my dreams, I dream of joy.
Ich
I
Kybd.
f

40
V.
bin im Schlaf so froh. Ich bin im Schlaf so froh.
am filled with joy. In my dreams I am filled with joy.
Kybd.
non leggiero
42
(I am filled with joy I am filled with joy).
45
Ich bin im Schlaf so froh, so froh, so
In my dreams I am filled with joy, with
molto crescendo
leggiero poco ritard
leggiero

Mein Leben hängt von Nacht zu Nacht,
von Schlaf zu Schlaf, von Traum zu Traum.
O rafft mich nicht aus mir Empor.
Ich bin im Schlaf so froh.
Ich bin im Schlaf so froh!

I live my life from night to night,
from sleep to sleep, from dream to dream.
O, do not wake me out of my dream.
I am filled with joy in my dreams.
In my dreams I dream of joy!

In Memory of Samuel Rosenbaum

Dear Friend

Magaht Sofir

Samuel Adler

13
V.
high-er than those packs of ci-gar-ettes we shared back then, nor big-ger than my hand.
Kybd.
16
Com-plete - ly dis - pro - por - tion-ate
19
these things which I can hold, so few com-pared to what I car-ry a-round in-
22
side not pos-sib-ly con - tained in a - ny case of a - ny shape

V.
ex-pand-ing out like rays which light my face when I've been stirred;
Kybd.
you through word or touch.
You've said as much
and said so much
ac-tions speak lou-der than words
(we learned when
we were learn - ing all these ax-ioms of life).
I can on - ly let

V.
soar my fan - ta - sies
of what could have been,
might have...,
wish I'd...
you.
Kybd.
E-ven back then
I
al-ways knew
I
was on-ly there
in the in - ter - im.
8vb

High Voice

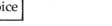

To Carol and Stuart Nelkin

I Will Betroth Thee

(V'eirastich Li)

Hosea 2: 21, 22
Song of Songs 2: 13

Samuel Adler

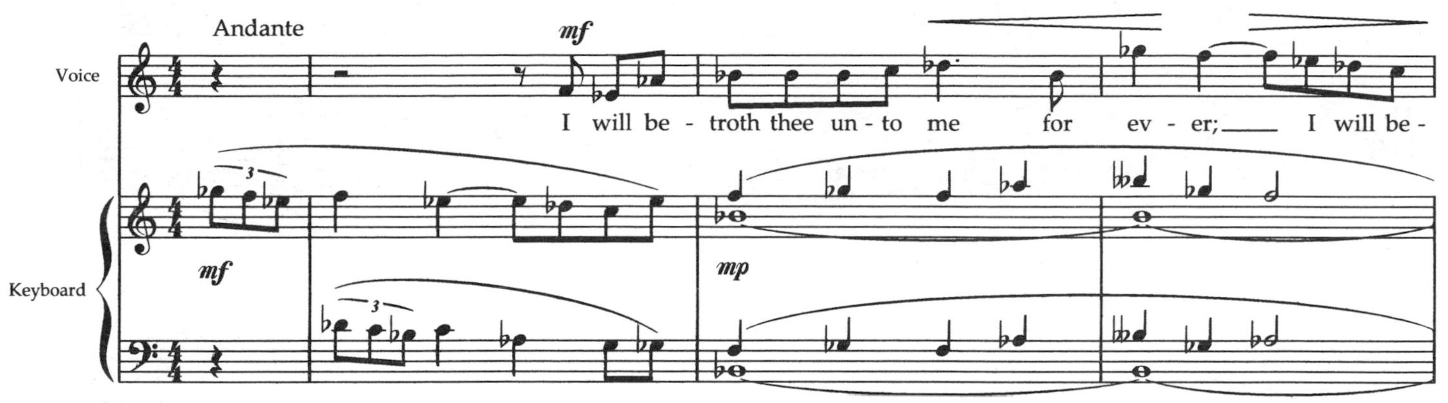

[N.B. Since this accompaniment was originally composed for organ, some of the lower octave notes may be played up one octave when using a piano or other keyboard (i.e., bars 6, 8, 9, etc.)]

V.
come a-way.
I will be-
Kybd.
troth thee un-to me in lov-ing-kind-ness, and in com-pas-sion.
I will be-troth thee un-to me,
I will be-troth thee un-to me in faith-ful-

24
V.
ness. And to-geth-er, yea to-geth-er we shall know the Lord,
Kybd.
27
to-geth-er we shall know the Lord.
3
mp
mf
mp

Dedicated to my twin grandsons, Benjamin and Ari Adler Beal

High Voice

Numi, Numi

(Sleep, Sleep)

Yechiel Heilperin
A Hebrew Lullaby

Yoel Engel
Arrangement by Samuel Adler

14
V.
dah, ha-lach, ha - lach a - ba. Ya-shuv, ya - shuv im tseit ha-l'-va-
Kybd.
f
18
nah ya-vi lach ma - ta - nah.
ritard
mf
As at the beginning (♩= 60)
22
mp
Nu - mi, nu - mi yal - da - ti. Nu - mi, nu - mi nim.
p
pp
26
pp
molto ritard
Nu - mi, nu - mi k'ta - na - ti. Nu - mi, nu - mi nim.
pp

נוּמִי, נוּמִי, יַלְדָּתִי
נוּמִי, נוּמִי נִים.
נוּמִי, נוּמִי, חֶמְדָּתִי,
נוּמִי, נוּמִי נִים.

אַבָּה הָלַךְ לָעֲבוֹדָה-
הַלָךְ, הַלָךְ אַבָּה.
יָשׁוּב עִם צֵאת הַלְּבָנָה
יַבִיא לָךְ מָתָּנָה.

Sleep, sleep, my little child.
Sleep, sleep.
Sleep, sleep, my little one,
Sleep, sleep.

Daddy's gone to work,
he went, Daddy went.
He'll return when the moon comes out,
he'll bring you a present.
Sleep, sleep . . .

High Voice

Dedicated to Andrew J. Isaacson on the occasion of his Bar Mitzvah

O God, I Believe in You So Much

Israel Emiot

Samuel Adler

Slowly, gently moving (♩ = 66)
Voice
Keyboard
mf
f
O God, my God, I ___ be-lieve in You ___ so much, be-lieve in

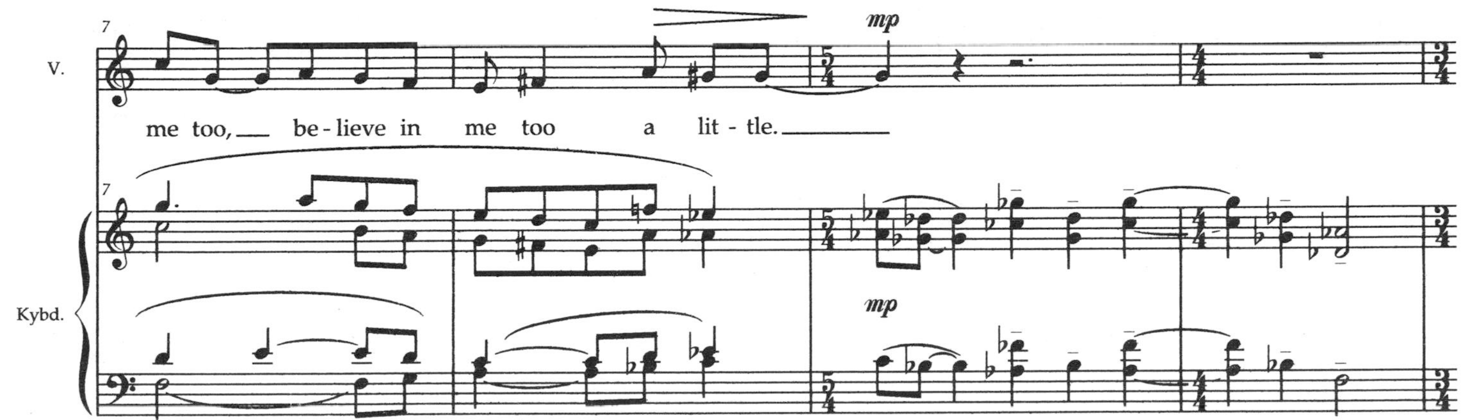
V.
Kybd.
mp
me too, ___ be-lieve in me too a lit - tle. ___

A bit more forward moving (but not fast) (♩ = 72)
V.
Kybd.
f
mf
How of - ten, how of - ten God You ___ try me! ___ Tough - en my spir -

ritard
mf
V.
- it. The curse I must wear was ne - ver fit-ted to my sta - ture;
Kybd.
mp
f
Whe - ther I rise or fall, whe - ther I rise or fall let it be true to my
mf
mea - sure. I did not ask to be great Nor the mean-est in cre - a - tion.
Yet you per - mit me but one ray to pierce the win - dow of my

Like the beginning
V.
pri-son. You who made ho-ly my mind, keep me from
Kybd.
join-ing Your be-tray-ers. Af-ter all, You cared when you as-signed co-lors to the
flo-wers. And when you pu-nished the night You did not o-ver pour:
And when You cursed the sea with tem-pests, You al-so chained it to the shore.

Relax the tempo to slower than the beginning (♩ = 52)
mf
V.
O God my God I be-lieve in You so much
Kybd.
mp
I be-lieve in You so much be-lieve in me, be-lieve in me
mp
mf
ritard
too, a lit-tle.

High Voice

Sand und Sterne

(Sand and Stars)

German translation (from the original Yiddish) by Shimon Frug
English Setting by Samuel Rosenbaum

Hugo Ch. Adler

Andante
Voice
Keyboard
p
Es leucht - et der Mond, die
The moon - light shines bright, the
6
V.
Kybd.
Ster - ne er - glä - zen, die Nacht schwebt nie - der auf Berg und Tal.
stars glow and glim - mer as dark - ness falls o - ver hill and glen.
piu mosso
ff
10
A Tempo
mf
Vor mir liegt das al - te
Be - fore me the ho - ly
calando

15
V.
Buch auf-ge-schla-gen, ich le - se und
Book lies o - pen, I read it, and
Kybd.
mf
19
le - se zum tau-send-sten mal, ich le - se die teu-e-ren, die
read it for the hund-redth and one time. I pon - der the pro - mise, the
p
poco
p
poco slargando
f
22
hei-li-gen Worte, und hör ei - ne Stim - me, ei - ne Stim - me: "Ich
sa - cred pro - mise, and up from the pag - es I hear an an-cient voice: "My

schwö - re, mein Volk, du wirst sein, wie die Ster - ne am
peo - ple, my peo - ple you will be as the stars in the
poco
Himmel, wie Sand am U - fer der Mee - re!"
hea - vens, as the sands at the edge of the sea."
Moderato
dolce
molto crescendo
ritard
Maestoso
Schöp - fer der Welt, von
Lord of the world, I
8va
V.
Kybd.

39
V.
dei - nen Schwü - ren kann nicht ver - fal - len ein
know full well, not a word of your pledge will ev - er
Kybd.
p
pp
43
ein - zi - ges Wort; er - füllt wer - den muss dein
be for - got - ten, ful - filled will be each word of Your
8vb
46
hei - li - ger Wil - le, al - les kommt zur Zeit, al - les
glo - ri - ous pro - mise all will be ful - filled in time, all will
(8vb)
3

49
V.
ritard
A Tempo
kommt zur Zeit und an sei - nem Ort.
be ful-filled in the right time and in the right place.
Kybd.
ff
molto crescendo
53
Und ei - nes ist schon er - füllt, er - füllt und ge -
And one vow has been ful - filled, ful-filled and come
ff mp
diminuendo
p
pp
57
sche - hen, das fühl ich bei je - dem Schritt: Wir sind
true. I feel it at ev - 'ry step: We have be-
p
p

61
V.
vo - gel-frei wie der Sand am Mee-re, wie der Sand am Mee - re, den je-der mit
come as sand at the edge of the sea, as sand at the sea-shore which all can
Kybd.
65
Andante molto
Füs - sen tritt Mein Gott wahr -
crush un-der foot. My God sure-ly
70
ritard
piu mosso
f
haf-tig wie Sand und Ster - ne, ver - streut und ver-wor-fen, ver-
we are like sand and like stones at the shore, scat - tered, up-root - ed and
p leggiero

V.
streut und ver - wor - fen zu Schan - de und Spott...
marked to be scorned and de - famed and a - bused...
Kybd.
piu mosso
loco
Tempo primo
A - ber die Ster - ne, die lich - ten, die
But where are the stars which you pro - mised
kla - ren, die Ster - ne, die Ster - ne, wo blei - ben sie,
would shine bright, the bright stars, the bright stars, where are the stars,
tenuto

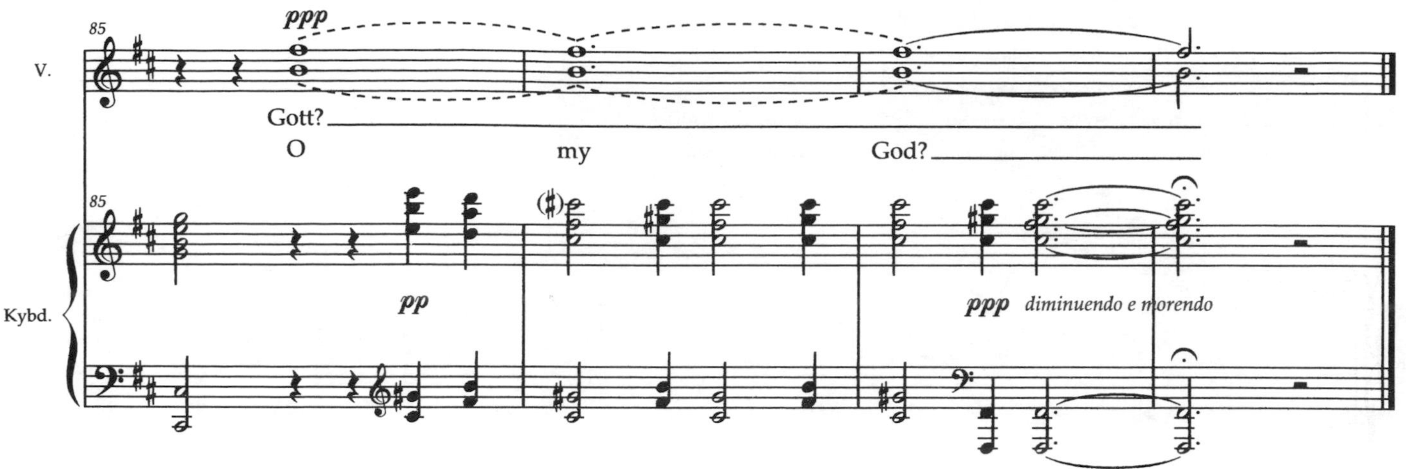

Es leuchtet der Mond, die Sterne erglänzen, die Nacht schwebt nieder auf Berg und Tal. Vor mir liegt das alte Buch aufgeschlagen, ich lese und lese zum tausendsten mal, ich lese die teueren, die heiligen Worte, und hör eine Stimme, eine Stimme: "Ich schwöre, mein Volk, du wirst sein, wie die Sterne am Himmel, wie Sand am Ufer der Meere!" Schöpfer der Welt, von deinen Schwüren kann nicht verfallen ein einziges Wort; erfüllt werden muss dein heiliger Wille, alles kommt zur Zeit, alles kommt zur Zeit und an seinem Ort. Und eines ist schon erfüllt, erfüllt und geschehen, das fühl ich bei jedem Schritt: Wir sind vogelfrei wie der Sand am Meere, wie der Sand am Meere, den jeder mit Füssen tritt. Mein Gott wahrhaftig wie Sand und Sterne, verstreut und verworfen, verstreut und verworfen zu Schande und Spott . . . Aber die Sterne, die lichten, die klaren, die Sterne, die Sterne, wo bleiben sie, Gott?	The moonlight shines bright, the stars glow and glimmer as darkness falls over hill and glen. Before me the ancient Book lies open. I read it and read it for the hundredth and one time. I ponder the promise, the sacred words, and up from the pages I hear an ancient voice: "My people, my people, you will be as the stars in the heavens, as the sands at the edge of the sea!" Lord of the world, I know full well, not a word of your pledge will ever be forgotten. Fulfilled with be each word of Your sacred promise. All will be fulfilled in time. All will be fulfilled in the right time and in the right place. And one vow has been fulfilled and come true. I feel it at every step. We have become as sand at the edge of the sea, as sand at the seashore which all can crush underfoot. My God, surely we are like sand and like stars at the shore, scattered, uprooted and marked to be scorned and defamed and abused . . . But where are the stars which you promised would shine bright, the bright stars, the bright stars, where are the stars, O my God?

Schneider, Schuster, Krämer

(Tailor, Cobbler, Grocer)

German translation from the original Yiddish Folksong by Hugo Ch. Adler
English setting by Samuel Rosenbaum

Hugo Ch. Adler

V.
1. Welt hin - ein!
2. Welt hin - ein!
3. Welt hin - ein!
Kybd.
poco meno
mf
Sprich doch Schnei - der Herz lieb - ster und Gu - ter,
Sprich doch Schus - ter hast du was zu beis - sen
Sprich doch Krä - mer hast wo - mit zu Han - deln
f
p
gibt dir dei - ne Na - del ge - nug für Brot und But - ter?
kannst du, wenn dir's fehlt auch an Ke - dit las - sen?
hast du im La - den Ro - si - nen und Man-deln?

A Tempo
V.
Kybd.
1. Ich ma - che die Wo - che zwei Ta - ler und' nen
2. Gar nie - mand borgt - e mir nicht mal ei - ne
3. Ich ha - be im La - den viel Wa - re fur hen
Drei - er, ich es - se bloss Brot die But -
Zwie - bel, ich bin nur ein Schus - ter und lau -
Spott ich schlep - pe die Ar - mut und lo -
- - ter ist mir zu teu - er!
- - fe, und lau - fe oh - ne Stie - fell.
- - be, und lo - be Gott!
1., 2.
3.

1. Ich bin ein Schneiderlein,
lebe so, tagaus, tagein!
Lustig, lustig, lustig in die Welt hinein!
Sprich doch Schneider Herz liebster und Guter,
gibt dir deine Nadel genug für Brot und Butter?
Ich mache die Woche
zwei Taler und' nen Dreier,
ich esse bloss Brot die Butter ist mir zu teuer!

2. Ich bin ein Schusterlein,
lebe so, tagaus, tagein!
Lustig, lustig, lustig in die Welt hinein!
Sprich doch Schuster hast du was zu beissen,
kannst du, wenn dir's fehlt auch an Kedit lassen?
Gar niemand borgte
mir nicht mal eine Zwiebel,
ich bin nur ein Schuster und laufe, und laufe ohne Stiefell.

3. Ich bin ein Krämerlein,
lebe so tagaus, tagein!
Lustig, lustig, lustig in die Welt hinein!
Sprich doch Krämer hast womit zu Handeln,
hast du im Laden Rosinen und Mandein?
Ich habe im Laden viel Ware fur hen Spott ich
schleppe die Armut und lobe, und lobe Gott!

1. I am a tailor man,
Cut and sew, day in, day out!
Happy! Happy am I as the day is long!
Tell me tailor, gentle, cheerful tailor,
does your needle bring you enough for bread and butter?
I earn each week a dollar and a quarter,
and I eat dry, black bread and dream
about eating buttered bread.

2. I am a cobbler man,
Pound the nails, day in, day out!
Happy! Happy am I as the day is long!
Tell me cobbler, can you feed your children,
can you, when you need it, get some food on credit?
Not one will lend me not even a sniff of an onion,
I may be a cobbler but I walk around every day,
I walk around barefoot.

3. I am a grocer man,
Buy and sell, day in, day out!
Happy! Happy am I as the day is long!
Tell me grocer, tell me what you sell there,
do you have to sell me some raisins and some almonds?
I cannot sell you a single raisin or an almond,
not a penny to my name and I thank our God for that!

High Voice

Tailor, Cobbler, Grocer

(Schneider, Schuster, Krämer)

Yiddish Folksong
English setting by Samuel Rosenbaum

Hugo Ch. Adler

Allegro Leggiero
Keyboard
mf
V.
1. I ___ am a tai-lor man. Cut and sew, cut and sew, cut and sew, day in, day
2. I ___ am a cob-bler man. Pound the nails, pound the nails, pound the nails, day in, day
3. I ___ am a gro-cer man. Buy and sell, buy and sell, buy and sell, day in, day
Kybd.
out. Hap-py! Hap-py! Hap - py, hap-py am ___ I as the day
out. Hap-py! Hap-py! Hap - py, hap-py am ___ I as the day
out. Hap-py! Hap-py! Hap - py, hap-py am ___ I as the day

19
V.
1. is long.
2. is long.
3. is long.
Kybd.
poco meno
mf
24
Tell me tai - lor, gen - tle, cheer - ful tai - lor.
Tell me cob - bler, can you feed your child - ren?
Tell me gro - cer, tell me what you sell there.
f
p
29
Does your need - le bring you e - nough for bread and but - ter?
Can you, when you need it, get some food on cre - dit?
Do you have to sell me, some rai - sins and some al - monds?

A Tempo
V.
Kybd.
1. I earn, I earn each week a dol - lar and a
2. Not one will lend me e-ven a sniff of an
3. I can - not sell you a sin - gle
quar - ter, and I eat dry black bread and dream
on - ion! I may be a cob - bler but I walk a - round
rai - sin or an al - mond. Not a pen - ny to my name
I dream a - bout eat - ing but - ter.
ev - ery day, I walk a - round bare-foot.
and I thank our God for that!
p
1., 2.
3.

To my beloved daughter Marianne

High Voice

Shalom Rav

(Abundant Peace)

Liturgy

Hugo Ch. Adler

Poco lento
Voice
Keyboard
Sha - lom rav al Yis - ra - el a - m'- cha ta-
V.
Kybd.
sim l' - o - lam, ki at - ah hu Me - lech,
Me-lech A-don l' - chol ha - sha - lom, V' - tov b'-ei - ne - cha, v' -
p

שָׁלוֹם רָב עַל יִשְׂרָאֵל עַמְּךָ תָּשִׂים לְעוֹלָם,
כִּי אַתָּה הוּא מֶלֶךְ אָדוֹן לְכָל הַשָּׁלוֹם.
וְטוֹב בְּעֵינֶיךָ לְבָרֵךְ אֶת עַמְּךָ יִשְׂרָאֵל,
בְּכָל עֵת וּבְכָל שָׁעָה בִּשְׁלוֹמֶךָ.

Grant abundant peace of Israel Your people forever,
for You are the Sovereign God of all peace.
May it be pleasing to You to bless Your people Israel
in every season and moment with Your peace.

High Voice

Sim Shalom

(Grant Peace)

Liturgy

Samuel Adler

V.
Kybd.
chad b'-or pa-ne-cha, ki v'-or pa-ne-cha na-ta-ta la-nu, A-do-nai
E-lo-hei-nu, To-rat cha-yim v'-a-ha-vat che-sed,
utz'-da-kah uv'-ra-chah v'-ra-cha-mim v'-cha-yim, v'-sha-lom.
V'-tov b'-ei-ne-cha l'-va-reich et am-cha Yis-ra-el b'-chol eit uv'-
mf
f
mp
p

שִׂים שָׁלוֹם טוֹבָה וּבְרָכָה,חֵן וָחֶסֶד וְרַחֲמִים,
עָלֵינוּ וְעַל כָּל יִשְׂרָאֵל עַמֶּךָ.
בָּרְכֵנוּ, אָבִינוּ, כֻּלָּנוּ כְּאֶחָד בְּאוֹר פָּנֶיךָ,
כִּי באוֹר פָּנֶיךָ נָתַתָּ לָּנוּ, יְיָ אֱלֹהֵינוּ,
תּוֹרַת חַיִּים וְאַהֲבַת חֶסֶד,
וּצְדָקָה וּבְרָכָה וְרַחֲמִים וְחַיִּים וְשָׁלוֹם.
וְטוֹב בְּעֵינֶיךָ לְבָרֵךְ אֶת עַמְּךָ יִשְׂרָאֵל
בְּכָל עֵת וּבְכָל שָׁעָה בִּשְׁלוֹמֶךָ.
בָּרוּךְ אַתָּה יְיָ, הַמְבָרֵךְ אֶת עַמּוֹ יִשְׂרָאֵל בַּשָּׁלוֹם.

Grant peace, goodness and blessing, grace, kindness, and mercy, to use and to all Your people Israel. Bless us, our Creator, all of us together, through the light of Your Presence. Truly through the light of Your Presence, Adonai our God, You gave us a Torah of life -- the love of kindness, justice and blessing, mercy, life, and peace. May You see fit to bless Your people Israel, at all times, at every hour, with Your peace. Praised are You Adonai, who blesses Your people Israel with peace.

This page has intentionally been left blank.

Dedicated to my beloved grandson, Joshua Adler Beal

Sleep Now

High Voice

Traditional Folk Lyric transcribed by Samuel Adler
Lullaby based on a Czech Folk Song

Samuel Adler

Gently moving (♩ = 60)
Voice
Keyboard
mf
mp
Sleep now dear son, sleep my angel, sleep tight.
f
Moth - er and fa - ther are right by your side.
p
Sleep now dear son, sleep my an - gel, now sleep.
V.
Kybd.

V.
Kybd.
mp
Moth - er and fa - ther are close to your feet.
pp
Sleep now
my son, my loved one sleep tight.
mf
Moth - er and fa - ther are
right at your side.
p
Sleep now, rest now my darl - ing
son.
mp
Moth - er and fa - ther do love you ver - y much.
ritard

V'sham'ru

(The People of Israel)

Liturgy

Louis Lewandowski
Arrangement by Hugo Ch. Adler

V.
Kybd.
Bei - ni u'-vein b'-nei Yis-ra - el ot hi l'-o - lam, ki
shei - shet ya - mim a - sah A - do - nai et ha - sha - ma - yim v'-
et ha - a - retz, u'- va - yom ha - sh - vi - i sha -
vat va - yi - na - fash.
Ped.

וְשָׁמְרוּ בְנֵי יִשְׂרָאֵל אֶת הַשַּׁבָּת,
לַעֲשׂוֹת אֶת הַשַּׁבָּת לְדֹרֹתָם בְּרִית עוֹלָם.
בֵּינִי וּבֵין בְּנֵי יִשְׂרָאֵל אוֹת הִיא לְעוֹלָם,
כִּי שֵׁשֶׁת יָמִים עָשָׂה יְיָ אֶת הַשָּׁמַיִם וְאֶת הָאָרֶץ,
וּבַיּוֹם הַשְּׁבִיעִי שָׁבַת וַיִּנָּפַשׁ.

The People of Israel shall keep Shabbat, observing Shabbat throughout the ages as a covenant for all time. It is a sign for all time between Me and the people of Israel. For in six days Adonai made heaven and earth, and on the seventh day God ceased from work and was refreshed.

High Voice

Wiegenlied

(Lullaby)

From the Yiddish by Berth. Felwel

Hugo Ch. Adler

Fine
V.
Kybd.
1. fei - nes Krön - lein, schlaf ei lu l'ju.
2. ist dein Va - ter, schlaf ei lu l'ju.
3. Zuk - ker plätz - chen, schlaf ei lu l'ju.
4. bes - te Pil - le, schlaf ei lu l'ju.
p
pp
Un poco animato
1. sitzt dein Müt-ter-chen an der Wie - ge singt dem Kind ein Lied und weint.
2. ei da drü - ben, weisst du, Lieb - ling ist das Le - ben wun - - - der - süss,
3. Va - ter rührt für uns die Hän - de schickt will's Gott ein Brief - - - chen her,
espressivo
spä - ter, spä - ter
ü - berm Mee - re
Zwan - zig Dol - lar
con tenerezza
rit.
ppp
molto leggiero e espresivo

molto ritard
1. wirst du's wis - sen was das klei - ne Lied - chen meint.
2. weisst du Lieb - ling 'ist es wie im Pa - ra - dies.
3. und wir fah - ren gleich. mein Klein - od ü - bers Meers.
V.
Kybd.
pp
p
molto ritard

Repeat first verse to Fine.

1. Schlaf mein süsses kleines Söhnlein,
schlaf ei lu l'ju, schlaf mein Trost mein feines Krönlein,
schlaf ei lu l'ju, sitzt dein Mütterchen
an der Wiege singt dem Kind ein Lied und weint.
später, später wirst du's wissen was das
kleine Liedchen meint.

1. Close your eyes now my precious little one
and sleep, ai'lulu. Sleep, my pretty one, my life,
my crown, my dear one, sleep ai'lulu.
Mother's arms are near, sleep and do not fear.
Mother sings her baby to sleep with a lullaby and weeps.
Later, later when you are older you will understand my song and my tears.

2. Welt, ach weit ist Kindchens Vater,
schlaf ei lu l'ju, in Amerika ist dein Vater,
schalf ei lu l'ju, ei da drüben, weisst du,
Liebling ist das Leben wundersüss,
überm Meere weisst du Liebling
'ist es wie im Paradies.

2. Far, far away your father waits to hold you,
sleep ai'lulu. Far away in America he waits and dreams,
ai'lulu. One day soon he will bring us to join him there.
One day we will be together in that beautiful land.
Till we enter that garden of Eden, sleep,
my precious one, ai'lulu.

3. Jeden Tag gibt's Weissbrot, Schätzchen,
schlaf ei lu l'ju, und fürs Kindchen Zukker
plätzchen, schalf ei lu l'ju, Vater rührt für uns
die Hände schickt will's Gott ein Briefchen her,
Zwanzig Dollar und wir fahren gleich.
mein Kleinod übers Meers.

3. There will be white bread each day and sweets
for you to eat. Father labors long to bring us
over there to be with him, ai'lulu.
He has promised to send us soon a letter -
and twenty dollars, too, and we shall fly away to him.

4. Bis das Briefchen kommt fein stille,
schlaf ei lu l'ju, schlafen ist dle beste Pille,
schalf ei lu l'ju.

4. Till that sweet letter comes and we go to him,
sleep now my baby, ai'lulu.

High Voice

Lullaby
(Wiegenlied)

From the Yiddish by Berth. Felwel
English setting by Samuel Rosenbaum

Hugo Ch. Adler

Adagio, molto amabile (♩ = 80)
Voice
Keyboard
1. Close your eyes now my pre - cious lit - tle one and
2. Far, far far a - way your fa - ther waits to hold you
3. There will be white bread each day and
simile
sempre legato
sleep ah lu lu. Sleep, my pret - ty one, my
sleep ah lu lu. Far a - way in A -
sweets for you to eat. Fa - ther la - bors long to
V.
Kybd.
life, my crown, my dear one, sleep ah lu lu.
mer - i - ca he waits and dreams, al lu lu.
bring us o - ver there to be with him, ah lu lu.
Fine

Repeat first verse to Fine.

This page has intentionally been left blank.

This page has intentionally been left blank.

In memory of Sarah Tankus Weinberger

Low Voice

A Woman of Valor

(Eishet Chayil)

Proverbs 31:20, 28-30

Samuel Adler

Andantino (♩ = 58)
Voice
Keyboard
mf
mp
A wo-man of val - or who can find?
Her price is far a-bove ru - bies. Her child-ren rise up, and call her
bless-ed; her hus - band al - so, and he prais - es her. Man-y daugh - ters
V.
Kybd.

V.
Kybd.
have done val-iant-ly, But thou ex-cel-lest them all. Grace is de-ceit-ful, and
beau-ty is vain; but a wo - man that fear-eth the Lord, she shall be prais - ed,
she shall be prais-ed, she shall be prais - ed.
mp
p
f
mf
molto ritard

Low Voice

Ahavat Olam
(Everlasting Love)

Liturgy

Samuel Adler

V.
Kybd.
mei-nu na-si-ach b'-chu-ke-cha, v'-nis-mach b'-div-rei to-ra-te-cha uv'-mitz-vo-te-cha
l'-o-lam va-ed. Ki heim cha-yei-nu v'-o-rech ya-mei-nu u-va-
hem ne-h'-geh yo-mam va-lai-lah. V'-a-ha-va-t'-cha
al ta-sir mi-me-nu l'-o-la-mim. Ba-ruch a-tah, A-do-

אַהֲבַת עוֹלָם בֵּית יִשְׂרָאֵל עַמְּךָ אָהָבְתָּ,
תּוֹרָה וּמִצְוֹת, חֻקִּים וּמִשְׁפָּטִים, אוֹתָנוּ לִמַּדְתָּ.
עַל כֵּן יְיָ אֱלֹהֵינוּ, בְּשָׁכְבֵנוּ וּבְקוּמֵנוּ נָשִׂיחַ בְּחֻקֶּיךָ,
וְנִשְׂמַח בְּדִבְרֵי תוֹרָתֶךָ וּבְמִצְוֹתֶיךָ לְעוֹלָם וָעֶד.
כִּי הֵם חַיֵּינוּ וְאֹרֶךְ יָמֵינוּ, וּבָהֶם נֶהְגֶּה יוֹמָם וָלָיְלָה.
וְאַהֲבָתְךָ אַל תָּסִיר מִמֶּנּוּ לְעוֹלָמִים.
בָּרוּךְ אַתָּה יְיָ, אוֹהֵב עַמּוֹ יִשְׂרָאֵל.

Everlasting love You offered Your people Israel
by teaching us Torah and mitzvot, laws and precepts.
Therefore, Adonai our God,
when we lie down and when we rise up,
we will meditate on Your laws and Your commandments.
We will rejoice in Your Torah for ever.
Day and night we will reflect on them
for they are our life and doing them lengthens our days.
Never remove Your love from us.
Praise to You, Adonai, who loves Your people Israel.

Low Voice

Bitte

(Plea)

German translation (from original Yiddish) by Albert Ehrenstein
English setting by Samuel Rosenbaum

Hugo Ch. Adler

Molto moderato
Keyboard
mf
p
calmo
V.
Mein_ Le - ben_ hängt von_ Nacht_ zu_ Nacht, von_ Schlaf
I_ like_ my_ life from_ night_ to_ night, from_ sleep
Kybd.
ritard
pp
zu Schlaf, von Nacht zu_ Nacht, von Schlaf zu_ Schlaf, von
to sleep, from night to_ night, from sleep to_ sleep, from

V.
Kybd.
pp
diminuendo
Traum zu Traum, von Traum zu
dream to dream, from dream to
diminuendo
Piu lento e maestoso
f
Traum.
dream.
O rafft mich
O do not
p
molto crescendo
ff
poco ritard
f
8vb
nicht aus mir em - por, o rafft mich nicht aus mir em -
wake me out of my dream, o do not wake me out of my
8vb

molto diminuendo
A tempo
V.
por, ich bin, ich bin im Schlaf so froh.
dream, I am filled with joy in my dreams.
Kybd.
Un poco piu mosso
Ich bin im Schlaf so froh. Ich
In my dreams I am filled with joy. In my
(leggiere)
bin im Schlaf so froh.
dreams I am filled with joy.

V.
(filled with joy, filled with joy, filled with joy, filled with joy)
Kybd.
p
pp
Ich bin im Schlaf so froh. Ich
I am filled with joy, in my dreams. In my
bin im Schlaf so froh. Ich bin im Schlaf so froh. Ich
dreams, I dream of joy. In my dreams, I dream of joy. I
f

V.
bin im Schlaf so froh. Ich bin im Schlaf so froh.
am filled with joy. In my dreams I am filled with joy.
Kybd.
non leggiero
V.
(I am filled with joy I am filled with joy).
Kybd.
V.
molto crescendo
Ich bin im Schlaf so froh, so froh, so
In my dreams I am filled with joy, with
Kybd.
leggiero poco ritard
leggiero

Mein Leben hängt von Nacht zu Nacht,
von Schlaf zu Schlaf, von Traum zu Traum.
O rafft mich nicht aus mir Empor.
Ich bin im Schlaf so froh.
Ich bin im Schlaf so froh!

I live my life from night to night,
from sleep to sleep, from dream to dream.
O, do not wake me out of my dream.
I am filled with joy in my dreams.
In my dreams I dream of joy.

Low Voice

To Carol and Stuart Nelkin

I Will Betroth Thee

(V'eirastich Li)

Hosea 2: 21, 22
Song of Songs 2: 13

Samuel Adler

[N.B. Since this accompaniment was originally composed for organ, some of the lower octave notes may be played up one octave when using a piano or other keyboard (i.e., bars 6, 8, 9, etc.)]

V.
come a-way.
I will be-
troth thee un-to me in lov-ing-kind-ness, and in com-pas-sion.
I will be-troth thee un-to me,
I will be-troth thee un-to me in faith-ful-
Kybd.
f
mf
mp
(f)

V.
ness. And together, yea together we shall know the Lord,
Kybd.
V.
together we shall know the Lord.
mp
mf
mp
Kybd.

Dedicated to my twin grandsons, Benjamin and Ari Adler Beal

Low Voice

Numi, Numi

(Sleep, Sleep)

Yechiel Heilperin
A Hebrew Lullaby

Yoel Engel
Arrangement by Samuel Adler

V.
Kybd.
dah, ha-lach, ha - lach a - ba.
Ya-shuv, ya - shuv im tseit ha-l'-va-
nah ya-vi lach ma - ta - nah.
ritard
As at the beginning (♩ = 60)
Nu - mi, nu - mi yal - da - ti.
Nu - mi, nu - mi nim.
molto ritard
Nu - mi, nu - mi k'ta - na - ti.
Nu - mi, nu - mi nim.

נוּמִי, נוּמִי, יַלְדָּתִי
נוּמִי, נוּמִי נִים.
נוּמִי, נוּמִי, חֶמְדָּתִי,
נוּמִי, נוּמִי נִים.

אַבָּא הָלַךְ לָעֲבוֹדָה-
הָלַךְ, הָלַךְ אַבָּא.
יָשׁוּב עִם צֵאת הַלְּבָנָה
יָבִיא לָךְ מַתָּנָה.

Sleep, sleep, my little child.
Sleep, sleep.
Sleep, sleep, my little one,
Sleep, sleep.

Daddy's gone to work,
he went, Daddy went.
He'll return when the moon comes out,
he'll bring you a present.
Sleep, sleep . . .

Low Voice

Dedicated to Andrew J. Isaacson on the occasion of his Bar Mitzvah

O God, I Believe in You So Much

Israel Emiot

Samuel Adler

Slowly, gently moving (♩ = 66)
Voice
Keyboard
mf
f
O God, my God, I ___ be-lieve in You so much, be - lieve in
V.
Kybd.
me too, __ be-lieve in me too a lit - tle. ____
mp
A bit more forward moving (but not fast) (♩ = 72)
How of - ten, how of-ten God You __ try me! ___ Tough - en my spir -

ritard
V.
Kybd.
- it. The curse I must wear was ne - ver fit-ted to my sta - ture;
Whe-ther I rise or fall, whe-ther I rise or fall let it be true to my
mea-sure. I did not ask to be great Nor the mean-est in cre - a - tion.
Yet you per - mit me but one ray to pierce the win - dow of my

Like the beginning
V.
Kybd.
prison. You who made holy my mind, keep me from
joining Your betrayers. After all, You cared when you assigned colors to the
flowers. And when you punished the night You did not over pour:
And when You cursed the sea with tempests, You also chained it to the shore.

Relax the tempo to slower than the beginning (♩ = 52)
V.
Kybd.
O God my God I be-lieve in You so much
I be-lieve in You so much be-lieve in me, be-lieve in me
too, a lit-tle.
ritard
mf
mp

Low Voice

Sand und Sterne

(Sand and Stars)

German translation (from the original Yiddish) by Shimon Frug
English Setting by Samuel Rosenbaum

Hugo Ch. Adler

Andante
Voice
Keyboard
p
Es leucht - et der Mond, die
The moon-light shines bright, the
V.
Kybd.
Ster - ne er - glä - zen, die Nacht schwebt nie - der auf Berg und Tal.
stars glow and glim-mer as dark - ness falls o - ver hill and glen.
piu mosso
ff
A Tempo
mf
Vor mir liegt das al - te
Be - fore me the ho - ly
calendo

15
V.
Buch auf-ge-schla-gen,
Book lies o-pen,
ich le - se und
I read it, and
Kybd.
mf
19
le - se zum tau-send-sten mal,
read it for the hund-redth and one time.
ich le - se die teu-e-ren, die
I pon - der the pro - mise, the
p
poco
p
22
poco slargando
f
hei-li-gen Worte, und hör ei - ne Stim - me, ei - ne Stim - me: "Ich
sa - cred pro - mise, and up from the pag - es I hear an an-cient voice: "My

26
V.
f
schwö - re, mein Volk, du wirst sein, wie die Ster - ne am
peo - ple, my peo - ple you will be as the stars in the
Kybd.
f
poco
30
Him - mel, wie Sand am U - fer der Mee - re!"
hea - vens, as the sands at the edge of the sea."
Moderato
dolce
f
molto crescendo
35
ritard
Maestoso
f
Schöp - fer der Welt, von
Lord of the world, I
8va
mf

39
V.
dei - nen Schwü - ren kann nicht ver - fal - len ein
know full well, not a word of your pledge will ev - er
39
p
pp
Kybd.
43
V.
ein - zi - ges Wort; er - füllt wer - den muss dein
be for - got - ten, ful - filled will be each word of Your
43
Kybd.
8vb
46
V.
hei - li - ger Wil - le, al - les kommt zur Zeit, al - les
glo - ri - ous pro - mise all will be ful - filled in time, all will
46
Kybd.
3
(8vb)

ritard
A Tempo
V.
kommt zur Zeit und an sei-nem Ort.
be ful-filled in the right time and in the right place.
Kybd.
ff molto crescendo
V.
Und ei-nes ist schon er-füllt, er-füllt und ge-
And one vow has been ful-filled, ful-filled and come
Kybd.
ff mp diminuendo p pp
V.
sche-hen, das fühl ich bei je - dem Schritt: Wir sind
true. I feel it at ev - 'ry step: We have be-
Kybd.
p
p

61
V.
vo - gel-frei wie der Sand am Mee-re, wie der Sand am Mee - re, den je-der mit
come as sand at the edge of the sea, as sand at the sea-shore which all can
Kybd.
65
Andante molto
Füs - sen tritt Mein Gott wahr -
crush un-der foot. My God sure - ly
70
ritard
piu mosso
f
haf-tig wie Sand und Ster - ne, ver - streut und ver-wor-fen, ver-
we are like sand and like stones at the shore, scat - tered, up-root - ed and
p leggiero

75
V.
streut und ver - wor - fen zu Schan - de und Spott . . .
marked to be scorned and de - famed and a - bused . . .
Kybd.
piu mosso
8va
8vb
loco
Tempo primo
78
p
A - ber die Ster - ne, die lich - ten, die
But where are the stars which you pro - mised
(8va)
(8vb)
81
ff
tenuto
kla - ren, die Ster - ne, die Ster - ne, wo blei - ben sie,
would shine bright, the bright stars, the bright stars, where are the stars,
pf

Es leuchtet der Mond, die Sterne erglänzen,	The moonlight shines bright, the stars glow
die Nacht schwebt nieder auf Berg und Tal.	and glimmer as darkness falls over hill and glen.
Vor mir liegt das alte Buch aufgeschlagen,	Before me the ancient Book lies open.
ich lese und lese zum tausendsten mal,	I read it and read it for the hundredth and one time.
ich lese die teueren, die heiligen Worte,	I ponder the promise, the sacred words,
und hör eine Stimme, eine Stimme:	and up from the pages I hear an ancient voice:
"Ich schwöre, mein Volk, du wirst sein,	"My people, my people,
wie die Sterne am Himmel,	you will be as the stars in the heavens,
wie Sand am Ufer der Meere!"	as the sands at the edge of the sea!"
Schöpfer der Welt, von deinen Schwüren	Lord of the world, I know full well,
kann nicht verfallen ein einziges Wort;	not a word of your pledge will ever be forgotten.
erfüllt werden muss dein heiliger Wille,	Fulfilled with be each word of Your sacred promise.
alles kommt zur Zeit, alles kommt zur Zeit	All will be fulfilled in time.
und an seinem Ort.	All will be fulfilled in the right time and in the right place.
Und eines ist schon erfüllt,	And one vow has been fulfilled and come true.
erfüllt und geschehen,	I feel it at every step.
das fühl ich bei jedem Schritt:	We have become as sand at the edge of the sea,
Wir sind vogelfrei wie der Sand am Meere,	as sand at the seashore which all can crush underfoot.
wie der Sand am Meere, den jeder mit Füssen tritt.	My God, surely we are like sand and like stars at the shore,
Mein Gott wahrhaftig wie Sand und Sterne,	scattered, uprooted and marked to be scorned
verstreut und verworfen,	and defamed and abused . . .
verstreut und verworfen zu Schande und Spott . . .	But where are the stars which you promised
Aber die Sterne, die lichten, die klaren,	would shine bright, the bright stars, the bright stars,
die Sterne, die Sterne, wo bleiben sie, Gott?	where are the stars, O my God?

Schneider, Schuster, Krämer

(Tailor, Cobbler, Grocer)

German translation from the original Yiddish Folksong by Hugo Ch. Adler
English setting by Samuel Rosenbaum

Hugo Ch. Adler

19
V.
1. Welt hin - ein!
2. Welt hin - ein!
3. Welt hin - ein!
19
Kybd.
24
poco meno
mf
V.
Sprich doch Schnei - der Herz lieb - ster und Gu - ter,
Sprich doch Schus - ter hast du was zu beis - sen
Sprich doch Krä - mer hast wo - mit zu Han - deln
24
Kybd.
f
p
29
V.
gibt dir dei - ne Na - del ge - nug für Brot und But - ter?
kannst du, wenn dir's fehlt auch an Ke - dit las - sen?
hast du im La - den Ro - si - nen und Man-deln?
29
Kybd.

A Tempo
V.
Kybd.
1. Ich ma - che die Wo - che zwei Ta - ler und' nen
2. Gar nie - mand borgt - e mir nicht mal ei - ne
3. Ich ha - be im La - den viel Wa - re fur hen
Drei - er, ich es - se bloss Brot die But -
Zwie - bel, ich bin nur ein Schus - ter und lau -
Spott ich schlep - pe die Ar - mut und lo -
- - ter ist mir zu teu - er!
- - fe, und lau - fe oh - ne Stie - fell.
- - be, und lo - be Gott!
1., 2.
3.

1. Ich bin ein Schneiderlein,
lebe so, tagaus, tagein!
Lustig, lustig, lustig in die Welt hinein!
Sprich doch Schneider Herz liebster und Guter,
gibt dir deine Nadel genug für Brot und Butter?
Ich mache die Woche
zwei Taler und' nen Dreier,
ich esse bloss Brot die Butter ist mir zu teuer!

2. Ich bin ein Schusterlein,
lebe so, tagaus, tagein!
Lustig, lustig, lustig in die Welt hinein!
Sprich doch Schuster hast du was zu beissen,
kannst du, wenn dir's fehlt auch an Kedit lassen?
Gar niemand borgte
mir nicht mal eine Zwiebel,
ich bin nur ein Schuster und laufe, und laufe ohne Stiefell.

3. Ich bin ein Krämerlein,
lebe so tagaus, tagein!
Lustig, lustig, lustig in die Welt hinein!
Sprich doch Krämer hast womit zu Handeln,
hast du im Laden Rosinen und Mandein?
Ich habe im Laden viel Ware fur hen Spott ich
schleppe die Armut und lobe, und lobe Gott!

1. I am a tailor man,
Cut and sew, day in, day out!
Happy! Happy am I as the day is long!
Tell me tailor, gentle, cheerful tailor,
does your needle bring you enough for bread and butter?
I earn each week a dollar and a quarter,
and I eat dry, black bread and dream
about eating buttered bread.

2. I am a cobbler man,
Pound the nails, day in, day out!
Happy! Happy am I as the day is long!
Tell me cobbler, can you feed your children,
can you, when you need it, get some food on credit?
Not one will lend me not even a sniff of an onion,
I may be a cobbler but I walk around every day,
I walk around barefoot.

3. I am a grocer man,
Buy and sell, day in, day out!
Happy! Happy am I as the day is long!
Tell me grocer, tell me what you sell there,
do you have to sell me some raisins and some almonds?
I cannot sell you a single raisin or an almond,
not a penny to my name and I thank our God for that!

Low Voice

Tailor, Cobbler, Grocer

(Schneider, Schuster, Krämer)

Yiddish Folksong
English setting by Samuel Rosenbaum

Hugo Ch. Adler

Allegro Leggiero
Keyboard
mf
V.
mf
1. I__ am a tai-lor man. Cut and sew, cut and sew, cut and sew, day in, day
2. I__ am a cob-bler man. Pound the nails, pound the nails, pound the nails, day in, day
3. I__ am a gro-cer man. Buy and sell, buy and sell, buy and sell, day in, day
Kybd.
V.
out. Hap-py! Hap-py! Hap - py, hap-py am__ I as the day
out. Hap-py! Hap-py! Hap - py, hap-py am__ I as the day
out. Hap-py! Hap-py! Hap - py, hap-py am__ I as the day
Kybd.

19
V.
1. is long.
2. is long.
3. is long.
Kybd.
24
poco meno
mf
Tell me tai - lor, gen - tle, cheer - ful tai - lor.
Tell me cob - bler, can you feed your child - ren?
Tell me gro - cer, tell me what you sell there.
f
p
29
Does your need - le bring you e - nough for bread and but - ter?
Can you, when you need it, get some food on cre - dit?
Do you have to sell me, some rai - sins and some al-monds?

34
A Tempo
V.
1: I earn, I earn each week a dol - lar and a
2. Not one will lend me e-ven a sniff of an
3. I can - not sell you a sin - gle
Kybd.
p
39
quar - ter, and I eat dry black bread and dream
on - ion! I may be a cob - bler but I walk a - round
rai - sin or an al - mond. Not a pen - ny to my name
p
43
1., 2.
3.
I dream a - bout eat - ing but - ter.
ev - ery day, I walk a - round bare - foot.
and I thank our God for that!

To my beloved daughter Marianne

Low Voice

Shalom Rav

(Abundant Peace)

Liturgy

Hugo Ch. Adler

שָׁלוֹם רָב עַל יִשְׂרָאֵל עַמְּךָ תָּשִׂים לְעוֹלָם,
כִּי אַתָּה הוּא מֶלֶךְ אָדוֹן לְכָל הַשָּׁלוֹם.
וְטוֹב בְּעֵינֶיךָ לְבָרֵךְ אֶת עַמְּךָ יִשְׂרָאֵל,
בְּכָל עֵת וּבְכָל שָׁעָה בִּשְׁלוֹמֶךָ.

Grant abundant peace of Israel Your people forever,
for You are the Sovereign God of all peace.
May it be pleasing to You to bless Your people Israel
in every season and moment with Your peace.

Low Voice

Sim Shalom

(Grant Peace)

Liturgy

Samuel Adler

V.
Kybd.
mf
f
chad b'-or pa-ne - cha, ki v'-or pa-ne - cha na - ta - ta la - nu, A-do-nai
mp
mp
p
E-lo-hei - nu, To - rat cha-yim v' - a-ha-vat che - sed,
utz' - da-kah uv'-ra-chah v'-ra-cha-mim v'-cha - yim, v'-sha - - lom.
mf
p
V'-tov b' - ei - ne - cha l'-va-reich et am-cha Yis-ra - el b'-chol eit uv'-

שִׂים שָׁלוֹם טוֹבָה וּבְרָכָה,חֵן וָחֶסֶד וְרַחֲמִים,
עָלֵינוּ וְעַל כָּל יִשְׂרָאֵל עַמֶּךָ.
בָּרְכֵנוּ, אָבִינוּ, כֻּלָּנוּ כְּאֶחָד בְּאוֹר פָּנֶיךָ,
כִּי בְאוֹר פָּנֶיךָ נָתַתָּ לָּנוּ, יְיָ אֱלֹהֵינוּ,
תּוֹרַת חַיִּים וְאַהֲבַת חֶסֶד,
וּצְדָקָה וּבְרָכָה וְרַחֲמִים וְחַיִּים וְשָׁלוֹם.
וְטוֹב בְּעֵינֶיךָ לְבָרֵךְ אֶת עַמְּךָ יִשְׂרָאֵל
בְּכָל עֵת וּבְכָל שָׁעָה בִּשְׁלוֹמֶךָ.
בָּרוּךְ אַתָּה יְיָ, הַמְבָרֵךְ אֶת עַמּוֹ יִשְׂרָאֵל בַּשָּׁלוֹם.

Grant peace, goodness and blessing, grace, kindness, and mercy, to use and to all Your people Israel. Bless us, our Creator, all of us together, through the light of Your Presence. Truly through the light of Your Presence, Adonai our God, You gave us a Torah of life -- the love of kindness, justice and blessing, mercy, life, and peace. May You see fit to bless Your people Israel, at all times, at every hour, with Your peace. Praised are You Adonai, who blesses Your people Israel with peace.

This page has intentionally been left blank.

Dedicated to my beloved grandson, Joshua Adler Beal

Low Voice

Sleep Now

Traditional Folk Lyric transcribed by Samuel Adler
Lullaby based on a Czech Folk Song

Samuel Adler

Gently moving (♩ = 60)
Voice
Keyboard
mf
mp
Sleep now dear son, sleep my an - gel, sleep
6
V.
Kybd.
f
tight. Moth - er and fa - ther are right by your side.
11
p
Sleep now dear son, sleep my an - gel, now sleep.

V.
Kybd.
mp
pp
mf
p
ritard
Moth - er and fa - ther are close to your feet. Sleep now
my son, my loved one sleep tight. Moth - er and fa - ther are
right at your side. Sleep now, rest now my darl - ing
son. Moth - er and fa - ther do love you ver - y much.
993357

Low Voice

Wiegenlied
(Lullaby)

From the Yiddish by Berth. Felwel

Hugo Ch. Adler

V.
Fine
1. fei - nes Krön - lein, schlaf ei lu l'ju.
2. ist dein Va - ter, schlaf ei lu l'ju.
3. Zuk - ker plätz - chen, schlaf ei lu l'ju.
4. bes - te Pil - le, schlaf ei lu l'ju.
Kybd.
Un poco animato
1. sitzt dein Müt - ter - chen an der Wie - ge singt dem Kind ein Lied und weint.
2. ei da drü - ben, weisst du, Lieb - ling ist das Le - ben wun - der - süss,
3. Va - ter rührt für uns die Hän - de schickt will's Gott ein Brief - chen her,
espressivo
spä - ter, spä - ter
ü - berm Mee - re
Zwan - zig Dol - lar
con tenerezza
rit.
molto leggiero e espressivo

molto ritard
19
V.
1. wirst du's wis - sen was das klei - ne Lied - chen meint.
2. weisst du Lieb - ling 'ist es wie im Pa - ra - dies.
3. und wir fah - ren gleich. mein Klein - od ü - bers Meers.
Kybd.
pp
p
molto ritard
Repeat first verse to Fine.

1. Schlaf mein süsses kleines Söhnlein,
schlaf ei lu l'ju, schlaf mein Trost mein feines Krönlein,
schlaf ei lu l'ju, sitzt dein Mütterchen
an der Wiege singt dem Kind ein Lied und weint.
später, später wirst du's wissen was das
kleine Liedchen meint.

1. Close your eyes now my precious little one
and sleep, ai'lulu. Sleep, my pretty one, my life,
my crown, my dear one, sleep ai'lulu.
Mother's arms are near, sleep and do not fear.
Mother sings her baby to sleep with a lullaby and weeps.
Later, later when you are older you will understand my song and my tears.

2. Welt, ach weit ist Kindchens Vater,
schlaf ei lu l'ju, in Amerika ist dein Vater,
schaf ei lu l'ju, ei da drüben, weisst du,
Liebling ist das Leben wundersüss,
überm Meere weisst du Liebling
'ist es wie im Paradies.

2. Far, far away your father waits to hold you,
sleep ai'lulu. Far away in America he waits and dreams,
ai'lulu. One day soon he will bring us to join him there.
One day we will be together in that beautiful land.
Till we enter that garden of Eden, sleep,
my precious one, ai'lulu.

3. Jeden Tag gibt's Weissbrot, Schätzchen,
schlaf ei lu l'ju, und fürs Kindchen Zukker
plätzchen, schaf ei lu l'ju, Vater rührt für uns
die Hände schickt will's Gott ein Briefchen her,
Zwanzig Dollar und wir fahren gleich.
mein Kleinod übers Meers.

3. There will be white bread each day and sweets
for you to eat. Father labors long to bring us
over there to be with him, ai'lulu.
He has promised to send us soon a letter -
and twenty dollars, too, and we shall fly away to him.

4. Bis das Briefchen kommt fein stille,
schlaf ei lu l'ju, schlafen ist dle beste Pille,
schaf ei lu l'ju.

4. Till that sweet letter comes and we go to him,
sleep now my baby, ai'lulu.

This page has intentionally been left blank.

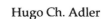

Low Voice

Lullaby

(Wiegenlied)

From the Yiddish by Berth. Felwel
English setting by Samuel Rosenbaum

Hugo Ch. Adler

Adagio, molto amabile (♩ = 80)
Voice
Keyboard
1. Close your eyes now my precious lit - tle one and sleep ah lu lu.
2. Far, far far a-way your fa - ther waits to hold you sleep ah lu lu.
3. There will be white bread each day and sweets for you to eat.
simile
sempre legato
Sleep, my pret - ty one, my life, my crown, my dear one, sleep ah lu lu.
Far a - way in A - mer - i - ca he waits and dreams, al lu lu.
Fa - ther la - bors long to bring us o-ver there to be with him, ah lu lu.
V.
Kybd.
Fine

993357

Un poco animato
V.
1. Moth-er's arms are near, sleep and do not fear. Moth-er sings her ba-by to sleep with a
2. One day soon he will bring us to join him there. One day we will be to-ge-ther
3. He has prom-ised to send us soon a let-ter and twen-ty dol-lars, too, will he send us and
Kybd.
pp
lu-la-by and weeps. Lat-er, lat-er
in that beau-ti-ful land. Till we en-ter that
we shall fly a-way to him. Till that sweet let-ter
espressivo
con tenerezza
ritard
ppp
molto leggiero e espressivo
when you are old-er you will un-der-stand my song and my tears.
gar-den of E-den sleep my pre-cious one, ah lu.
comes and we go to him, sleep now my ba-by, ah lu.
molto ritard
pp
p
Repeat first verse to Fine.

INDEX